What Kind of Family Is This?

A Book About Stepfamilies

By Barbara Seuling

Illustrated by Ellen Dolce

*Prepared with the cooperation of Bernice Berk, Ph.D.,
of the Bank Street College of Education*

A GOLDEN BOOK · NEW YORK
Western Publishing Company, Inc.   Racine, Wisconsin 53404

Note to Parents

When divorced parents remarry and join two families together, children often have fears about what their new family will be like. Sometimes they feel angry, ashamed, or sad. One of their biggest fears is that their own parent will spend less time with them and will love them less. Children may also be afraid that their new stepparent won't like them. Although sometimes this may be the case, usually it just takes time for everyone in a new family to get used to each other. It also takes time for love to grow.

WHAT KIND OF FAMILY IS THIS? can show your child that he or she is not the only one who has worries or uncertainties about becoming part of a new family. The best way to begin solving problems is to talk about them openly. Using WHAT KIND OF FAMILY IS THIS? as a starting point, you can encourage your child to talk about how he or she feels. When the lines of communication are open, you can identify the problems and go about solving them together—as a family.

—The Editors

Imagine if you were suddenly part of a whole new
family—with a new stepfather or stepmother, with a
new stepbrother, or a new stepsister, or even a new
stepbrother AND a new stepsister, and maybe even a new
pet or two—pets that didn't get along with your pet.

That's what it was like for Jeff when he moved in with
his new family. Jeff's mom and dad were divorced, which
was bad enough—but then his mom got married again!

There was Henry, Mom's new husband.

"Hello, son," said Henry.

Jeff didn't want Henry to call him "son." Jeff didn't want to call Henry "Dad," either, even though Henry was now officially his stepdad. So he just said, "Hello."

Besides, Jeff *had* a dad. Just because he didn't live with him anymore didn't mean Jeff didn't have one.

Jeff was *not* going to let Henry take his dad's place.

But there wasn't only Henry. Henry had two kids—
Scott and Samantha.

There were new rooms to sleep in, and eat in, and
wash in. Because there were so many people, there were
new rules to remember about chores, and TV, and talking
on the telephone, and even for using the bathroom.

This ended up in a lot of fights—like when Samantha, who was a teenager, was getting ready for a date, and Jeff had to wait outside the door to get in.

"**WHAT KIND OF FAMILY IS THIS?**" Jeff shouted one day. "I can't even go to the bathroom when I want to!"

Another problem was Jeff's room. It was not his room, exactly. It was Scott's old room, and Jeff had to share it with him.

Jeff was sitting on the bed one day, reading. Scott came in and banged his baseball glove down on the dresser. He turned on the radio—loud. Jeff got up to leave.

"Stay on your side of the room," said Scott.
"I *am* on my side of the room," said Jeff.
"Well, just be sure you stay there," Scott answered.
Then he pulled some string out of a drawer and tacked it
up, right down the middle of the room.
Jeff was angry. He stormed downstairs.

"WHAT KIND OF FAMILY IS THIS?" he shouted. "I don't have any privacy. I don't want to be here! Why do we have to live here anyway?"

Mom explained again that she and Henry loved each other and wanted to live together. She said they both loved their children, and they wanted to live with them too. The only way they could do that was for all of them to move in together, and learn to be a family *together*.

"It takes time, but you'll get used to it," she promised.
But Jeff was *not* getting used to it. He was sure he'd
never be used to it. As a matter of fact, he hated it.
Especially when he looked at that string dividing his
room in half.

Jeff was cleaning his gerbil cage one day when Squeaker got loose. The fat little gerbil scooted across the room.

"Squeaker! Come back!" called Jeff.

That's when Scott walked in, carrying his cat, Tiger.

Tiger leaped out of Scott's arms and Squeaker ran for the space under the dresser. He disappeared just in time.

"Get your cat out of here!" Jeff shouted. "He'll get Squeaker!"

"Maybe I should let him," said Scott. "After all, this used to be his room and mine. Tiger lived here first, before you and your old gerbil came to live here."

"We didn't ask to come here!" shouted Jeff.

Jeff watched in horror as Tiger scratched at the space under the dresser. "Hey! Stop that!" he said as he ducked under the string. He sat in front of the dresser, so Tiger couldn't get at Squeaker.

"Stay on your side of the room!" shouted Scott.

Jeff reached under the dresser and felt Squeaker's soft furry body trembling with fright. Scooping him up gently, Jeff brought him back to his cage on the other side of the room.

"Who wants to live in your old room anyway!" shouted Jeff, stroking Squeaker. "My room was ten times nicer than this. It was quiet, and neat, and had great posters on the wall, and...and...I even had my own private cave!"

Jeff hadn't really meant to tell that. It had been his secret.

Scott reached down and picked up Tiger. "What kind of cave?" he said, petting the cat.

Jeff stared down at Squeaker, who was curled up in his favorite corner. He was no longer trembling, and was munching a carrot slice. "It was really a closet," he said. "But I pretended it was a cave. I could make magical things happen there."

"Really?" said Scott. He put Tiger down. He went over to his closet and opened the door. "Look," he said. "If we took all this junk out of here, maybe this could be a cave. Come and see."

Jeff looked up. He wasn't sure he wanted to share his cave idea with Scott. Not after what he'd said about Squeaker. "No," he said. "It's on *your* side of the room."

Scott didn't hear. He was way inside his closet now, pitching out one thing after another...a pair of old cowboy boots, *thunk, thunk;* a baseball, *thwap;* a hockey stick, *clank;* a bicycle chain, *clang;* a rubber monster hand, *whap;* a Monopoly game, *rattle;* a pair of Mickey Mouse ears, *thwack;* a toy racing car set with tracks, *bonk;* a rolled-up canvas tent, *thud!*

Jeff took a look. It was a great closet. "This would make a terrific cave," he said, suddenly missing his old cave even more. Jeff felt like crying. He turned away, hoping Scott wouldn't see. Scott didn't. He was still deep inside the closet.

"Making a cave is a super idea," Scott said. "I didn't know you had any good ideas."

Just then Mom and Henry came in to see what the noise was all about.

"What's this?" said Henry, touching the string.

Scott looked embarrassed. He went over and pulled the string down. "Nothing," he said.

"What're you doing?" Mom asked.

Scott looked at Jeff. "Fixing up *our* room," he said.

Jeff was glad. "Can I put my spaceship poster on the wall?" he said.

"Sure," said Scott. "Maybe we should put it on the door. This could be our space station."

"Great idea," Jeff said. "I didn't know you had any good ideas, either."

The two boys smiled at each other.

After that day, Jeff and Scott sometimes fought and sometimes didn't. Sometimes they talked and sometimes they didn't. Scott told Jeff how he felt about having another mother. It was the same way Jeff felt about having another father—not so great, at first.

Jeff still didn't always get to the bathroom before Samantha, and sometimes he didn't get to watch the program he wanted on TV. He still had to listen to Scott's radio sometimes when he'd rather be reading. But just like his mom had promised, it was taking time, but he was beginning to get used to it.